DINOSAURS

p

This is a Parragon book
This edition published in 2005

Parragon
Queen Street House
4 Queen Street
Bath BA1 1HE, UK

ISBN 1-40545-638-8

Printed in China

Contents

Dinosaurs

The first dinosaurs appeared about 225 million years ago, and ruled the Earth for millions of years.

No one has ever seen a dinosaur alive, because they died out long before people appeared. But we know what they looked like, because scientists study their fossilized

bones to discover
the many weird
and wonderful
shapes and
sizes they
came in.

Plateosaurus

Herds of these large animals
travelled across the hot plains in
search of food. Plateosaurus walked
on all fours, but could rear up
on its hind legs to munch
leaves high on trees, using
its massive tail for support.

Herrerasaurus

Herrerasaurus was one of the first meat-eating dinosaurs, and was a fierce hunter with sharp teeth and claws. It ran at great speed on its powerful back legs, which helped it catch its prey.

Tyrannosaurus

The terrifying
Tyrannosaurus
towered as tall
as a small house.
The largest,
fiercest meat-eater,
it had huge jaws filled with
long, sharp teeth,
and its mouth
was big enough
to gulp you
down whole!

It ran upright on its powerful back legs, but its front legs were so short they couldn't reach its mouth. It carried its long tail upright as it moved, to balance the weight of its enormous body.

Lesothosaurus

These little dinosaurs lived in the desert in herds, grazing on the desert plants. They had nothing to defend themselves from predators with, but instead ran for cover at

high speed on their long back legs.
They would have been very difficult
to catch! They may have rested in
burrows during the hot summer until
the rains came again and there
was food to eat.

Diplodocus

Diplodocus was the longest dinosaur that ever lived.

It used its incredible neck to reach leaves high in the tree-tops. It had an even longer tail, which it may have used like a whip to scare away predators. It stayed in water for most of the time, out of reach of its fierce enemies.

Pteranodon

A Pteranodon's body was no bigger than a turkey's, but its great wings would have spread across a motorway.

It flew by gliding, rather than flapping its wings, and soared over the sea, snatching fish in its toothless jaws.

Archaeopteryx

Archaeopteryx was the first winged bird, but in many ways it was similar to the reptiles.

It had teeth, a long bony tail, proper clawed fingers on the front of its wings, and coloured feathers.

Stegosaurus

Stegosaurus was as long as a bus, but it only had a brain the size of a plum! It had bony

armour and two pairs of dangerous
spikes at the end of its tail. It
moved slowly on its four sturdy legs
and swallowed plants
without even chewing.

Allosaurus

Herds of Allosaurus are thought to have hunted together, feeding on other dinosaurs. They had powerful necks, sharp claws and strong wide-opening jaws. The Allosaurus' razor-sharp teeth made them deadly attackers.

 Minmi

The Minmi was one of the best protected dinosaurs. It had bony armour covering almost all of its body — even its belly.

Any dinosaur that tried to bite a
chunk out of Minmi risked breaking
some teeth!

Maiasaura

Maiasaura means "good mother lizard". About 20 eggs were laid in a large mud nest, then covered to keep them warm and protected. Dinosaur babies were very small and probably needed looking after for some time.

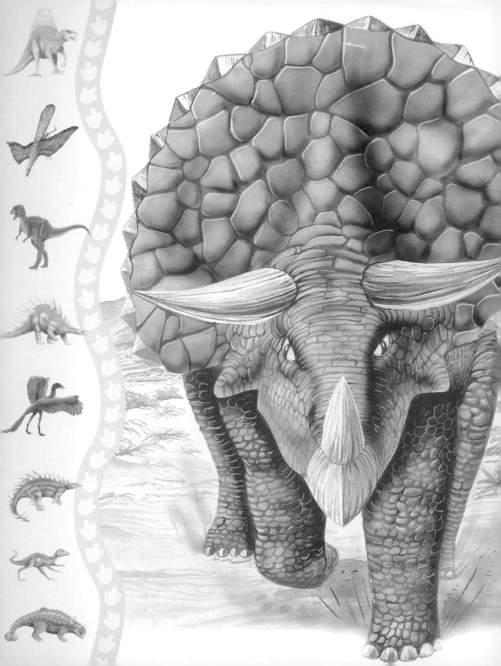

Triceratops

These great dinosaurs were among the last to appear on Earth and the last to die out. They thundered through the forests in large herds, made up of dozens of dinosaurs.

Saurolophus

This dinosaur had a bony spike on the back of its head, called a crest. It may have used this to make its noises louder, so it could warn others of danger. It could run away on two legs, and may have rushed into the water to escape predators.

Apatosaurus

Huge herds of plant-eating
Apatosaurus trundled along at
about the speed of elephants,
searching for food. The youngest
dinosaurs walked in the middle
of the herd, protected from
predators by the large adults.

Where did they go?

There are many suggestions of why the dinosaurs disappeared, but no real answers. Many scientists think a chunk of space rock smashed into Earth and threw up huge clouds of dust, blocking out the sun.

Without heat and light, the plants, plant-eaters and then meat-eaters would all have vanished. However the dinosaurs' descendants live on today — as our little feathered friends, the birds!